S0-AAA-751

BAD TIMES
IN HISTORY

Roland C. Barker

Gramercy Books
New York

Copyright © 2001 by Random House Value Publishing, Inc.

All rights reserved under International and Pan-American Conventions.

No part of this book may be reproduced or transmitted in any form or by any means, electronic or mechanical including photocopying, recording, or by any information storage and retrieval system, without permission in writing from the publisher.

This 2001 edition is published by Gramercy Books ™, an imprint of
Random House Value Publishing, Inc., 280 Park Avenue, New York, N.Y. 10017.

Gramercy Books™ and design are trademarks of Random House Value Publishing, Inc.

Random House
New York • Toronto • London • Sydney • Auckland
http://www.randomhouse.com/

Designed by Robert Yaffe

Printed and bound in the United States of America

On the cover: Atomic Bomb, August 8, 1945; Frenchman weeping as German soldiers march into Paris, June 14, 1940; San Francisco Earthquake, 1906 (Kingston, R.P./Index Stock Imagery)

Library of Congress Cataloging-in-Publication Data

Barker, Roland C.
    Bad days in history / Roland C. Barker.
        p. cm.
      ISBN 0-517-16264-4
        1. Disasters–History–Chronology. I. Title.

  D24 .B34 2001
  904–dc21

                                                                    00-057796

9 8 7 6 5 4 3 2 1

Richard Susan
4502 56th St. E.
Tacoma, WA 98443-2434

BAD TIMES
IN HISTORY

Early Times

54 AD Agrippina II poisoned Emperor Claudius so that her son, Nero, could become Emperor of Rome. Her constant political intrigues so annoyed her son that he had her murdered in 59 A.D.

64 AD A fire destroyed half of Rome, and Emperor Nero blamed the Christian population. Christians were gathered up, crucified, and burned alive.

70 AD The Romans, after a hundred years of occupation of Judea and more than four years of fighting revolts led by Jewish zealots, breached the walls of Jerusalem and destroyed the Second Temple. This was the final and most devastating Roman blow against Ancient Judea.

73 AD The Jews who had fled the Roman invasion of Jerusalem and stayed in the fortress of Masada, near the Dead Sea, committed mass suicide in order to avoid being taken by the Romans.

AUGUST 24, 79 AD Imperial Rome was at the height of its power when Mt. Vesuvius in Italy erupted, covering the town of Herculaneum with thick mud and obliterating Pompeii. The death toll was estimated at about 2,000.

NOVEMBER 1095   Pope Urban II called for the First Crusade. The first leaders departed in the summer of 1096. Dysentery soon broke out and killed more than 100,000 people, including German troops brought in as reinforcement.

1204   The Crusaders sacked Constantinople (Istanbul), massacring all its inhabitants.

MAY 20, 1277   Always a man of science as well as a priest, Pope John XXI built himself an observatory in the papal palace at Viterbo, Italy, where he could study the stars. One night in the spring of 1277, the roof collapsed on the Pope. The great beams crushed him, and on May 20, 1277, six days after the accident, Pope John XXI died.

The Renaissance

1337   The Hundred Years' War between England and France began when King Edward III of England invaded Normandy, France. This century-long series of conflicts was based on England's claim to the French throne and the trade rivalries between the two great Europeans powers.

1347   The first known outbreak of Bubonic Plague took place in the southern Ukraine near the Black Sea. During that same year, infected rats on a ship from the Crimea reached Sicily, and in March 1348, the Bubonic Plague struck in Florence, Italy, during which more than 96,000 people died until it ended in October. The plague spread throughout Europe in the Dark Ages, killing about half the population. It acquired the name "The Black Death" because of the black blotches on victims' bodies.

MARCH 15, 1391   On Ash Wednesday, arch-deacon Martinez of Seville incited his congregation to riot, and they attacked the city's Jewish quarter. This incident touched off the Spanish Inquisition, which lasted from then until the end of the fifteenth century.

MAY 31, 1431   Joan of Arc, now St. Joan, was burned at the stake as a heretic in Rouen, France.

1455   Start of the War of the Roses between the British House of Lancaster and the House of York for the throne of England.

1492   Christopher Columbus's arrival in the Dominican Republic marked the beginning of the demise of the Taino Indians. Disease brought by the Europeans caused death, there were massacres of the natives, and it is believed that many Tainos may have committed suicide because of the terrible conditions.

MARCH 31, 1492   King Ferdinand V and Queen Isabella announced their edict of expulsion of the Jews. Estimates of the number of Jews range from 165,000 to 400,000. About 50,000 Jews chose baptism to avoid expulsion.

JANUARY 3, 1521   Martin Luther was excommunicated from the Roman Catholic Church.

MAY 19, 1536   Anne Boleyn, the second wife of England's King VIII, failed to produce a male heir and was convicted of incest and adultery, and beheaded.

FEBRUARY 13, 1542   The fifth wife of England's King Henry VIII, Catherine Howard, was executed for adultery.

JANUARY 16, 1547   Ivan the Terrible was crowned Czar of Russia.

FEBRUARY 2, 1556 Probably the worst death toll by earthquake in history took place in China in Shaanxi. It is estimated that 830,000 people were killed when their cliff-like dwellings collapsed.

JANUARY 2, 1570 Tsar Ivan the Terrible began his march to Novgorod, and a week later 2,000 residents were killed.

1577 In England, as doctors struggled for new cures for illness, a  1571 report arrived from Spain, crediting the wonders of tobacco and its ability to cure 36 maladies. Tobacco was then recommended for toothache, falling fingernails, worms, halitosis, lockjaw, and cancer.

FEBRUARY 1, 1587 Queen Elizabeth I of England signed the death sentence for Mary Stuart, Queen of Scots.

FEBRUARY 17, 1598 Boris Godunov took over the Russian throne on the death of Fyodor I . At first a capable and benevolent ruler, fear of opposition led Boris to banish members of the Romanov family, set up a spy system and ruthlessly persecute his enemies. When he died in 1605 he left Russian in a state of civil war, foreign intervention, and social disorder—known as the Time of Troubles.

The Seventeenth Century

JANUARY 7, 1608 Fire destroyed Jamestown, Virginia.

JANUARY 30, 1649 England's King Charles the First was beheaded for treason.

JUNE 15, 1648 Margaret Jones, a Boston doctor who had lost several patients, became the first person executed as a witch in the Massachusetts Bay Colony.

SEPTEMBER 2, 1666 The Great Fire of London began accidentally in the house of the king's baker in Pudding Lane near London Bridge. Winds spread the fire and it destroyed a large part of the City of London, including most of the civic buildings, St. Paul's Cathedral, almost 100 churches, and about 13,000 homes.

1682 In the twelve years since the state of Virginia enacted a rule that Christians—including blacks— would not be liable to lifelong servitude, Virginia found that its stand on Christianity was cutting into the profits of slave owners. The 1670 law was repealed.

OCTOBER 18, 1685   Louis XIV of France revoked the Edict of Nantes (1598), which had assured all Protestants religious and civil liberties. Within a few years, more than 400,000 French Huguenots emigrated.

1669   The most violent eruption of Mt. Etna in Sicily occurred when about 990,000,000 cubic yards of lava were thrown out.

The Eighteenth Century

MAY 5, 1706   On Tenerife in the Canary Islands, the town of Guarrachici was destroyed by the eruption of Teide Volcano. People were buried alive, burned, asphyxiated, and crushed by a hail of enormous stones.

SEPTEMBER 1, 1730   Lanzarote, a volcano in the Canary Islands with a long history of eruption, began a new series of eruptions that continued until April, 1735 when the western quarter of the island was annihilated.

1770   The Great Famine of Bengal claimed the lives of 10 million Indians, about one-third of the population.

MARCH 5, 1770 The Boston Massacre occurred when British troops fired on a crowd they claimed to be unruly. The result was a bolstering of the revolutionary cause among patriots; 10,000 Bostonians (out of a population of 16,000) marched in the funeral procession of the victims.

APRIL 19, 1775 The exchange of gunfire between British soldiers and colonial militia at Lexington, Massachusetts, began the American Revolutionary War.

NOVEMBER 1, 1755 When Lisbon was struck by a series of earthquakes, the shocks were felt as far away as Scotland and Sweden. A third of the population of Lisbon died, approximately 50,000 people, and buildings toppled in neighboring Spain.

FEBRUARY 5, 1783 Earthquakes ravaged Calabria, Italy, killing 30,000.

SUMMER, 1783 Iceland lost about one-fifth of its population—about 10,000 people—following a

volcanic eruption of Mount Skaptar that covered 200 square miles and submerged 20 villages.

JULY 14, 1789   The Storm of the Bastille Prison in Paris began the French Revolution.

JANUARY 21, 1793   During the French Revolution, King Louis XVI and Queen Marie Antoinette, condemned for treason, were beheaded by the guillotine.

The Nineteenth Century

1812   Napoleon invaded Russia with his Grande Armée of 500,000.

1812   The Fort Dearborn Massacre occurred in Chicago during the War of 1812. Fort Dearborn, Michigan, under threat, was evacuated, but Indians attacked the evacuees. Many were massacred and the fort was destroyed.

1814   British troops took Washington, D.C. and burned the Capitol Building and the White House.

1817 A major outbreak of cholera occurred in Calcutta, India following a three-month festival that drew pilgrims from all over India. The disease spread throughout India, and according to British army statistics, 10,000 of their soldiers died. Based on this, it is assumed that hundreds of thousands of people died throughout India.

AUGUST 21, 1821 Nat Turner launched a bloody slave insurrection in Virginia, slaughtering his owner, his owner's family, and eventually killing 60 people. He was hanged on November 11.

OCTOBER 26, 1831 Cholera first hit England in the town of Sunderland. A quarantine of the ports, disastrous to the flourishing textile industry, was not put into effect because the disease was not considered contagious.

JANUARY 1834 The legislature of South Carolina passed a law prohibiting the teaching of black children, free or slave.

DECEMBER 16, 1835 New York City's greatest fire began in the Comstock & Adams dry goods store in lower Manhattan. It lasted 19 hours and burned 674 buildings south of Wall Street and east of Broadway, including the Merchants Exchange and the Custom House.

MARCH 6, 1836 The storming of the Alamo by the Mexicans ended a two-week siege. All Texans defending it were killed, including Davy Crockett, as well as 1600 Mexicans.

OCTOBER, 1837 A hurricane known as "Racer's Storm," which originated in Jamaica, wrecked three ships off the Outer Banks of North Carolina, drowning 90 of 130 passengers aboard the steamer *Home*. At least two other vessels were lost.

1837 First Opium War between Great Britain and China began. At the war's end in 1842, China ceded Hong Kong to the British.

1845 This year marked the start of the Irish Potato Famine.

1848   The Irish government closed the soup kitchens distributing free rations to the needy during the same year it had set them up. Responsibility was placed on local districts in Ireland, many of which were unable to provide the needed food.

JANUARY 16, 1848   The first reports arrived bearing the news of the Donner Party tragedy. George and Jacob Donner had left for California in the spring of 1847 as part of the Gold Rush and emigration to the West. They lost half of a party of 87 emigrants when they tried to cross the Sierra Nevada mountains before the winter snows, and failed. Survivors told stories of starvation and cannibalism.

APRIL 29, 1849   The emigrant boat *John Drew* docked in Chicago, bringing with it cholera. The epidemic raged until late October, killing 678. Cholera had killed more than 5,000 people in New York City in 1848.

AUGUST 24, 1857   The failure of the New York branch of the Ohio Life Insurance and Trust Company triggered the Panic of 1857, during which the New York Stock Exchange suffered collapse. Stocks fell up to 10 per cent in one day.

To make matters worse, the SS *Central America*, a sailing ship transporting millions of dollars in gold from the new San Francisco Mint to the East Coast, sank in September.

DECEMBER 2, 1859 Abolitionist John Brown was hanged for assaulting the U.S. arsenal at Harpers Ferry, a precursor to the Civil War.

JANUARY 9, 1861 In the first hostile act of the Civil War, the ship *Star of the West* fired on Fort Sumter, South Carolina.

MAY 1, 1863 Confederate troops fatally wounded Confederate general Thomas "Stonewall" Jackson, whom they had mistaken for a Yankee scout.

JULY 1, 1863 The beginning of the Battle of Gettysburg, considered the turning point of the Civil War. At the end of three days, there were combined casualties of 43,000. The death toll and the dedication of a national cemetery in Gettysburg in November 1863 were the basis for President Abraham's inspired Gettysburg Address.

1865 At the end of the Civil War, although slavery in the U.S. had been abolished, southern states instituted the Black Codes. These laws restricted the rights of freed blacks to bear arms, own property, assemble in public, hold certain jobs, or even travel without special passes. Although these codes were eventually struck down, they led the way for segregation and systematic discrimination of American blacks until the Civil Rights Movement in the 1950s.

APRIL 14, 1865 John Wilkes Booth shot President Lincoln while attending Ford's Theater in Washington, D.C. Lincoln died the following day.

APRIL 1865 At the end of the Civil War, it was discovered that Anderson Prison, an open-air Confederate prison in southwestern Georgia, had held more than 45,000 Union soldiers, a number well beyond its capacity. Thousands had died of disease and starvation. Captain Henry Wirz, Andersonville's commander, was convicted of war crimes and hanged on November 10, 1865, the only person to be executed as a result of the Civil War.

SEPTEMBER 6, 1869 One of the worst mining disasters of the nineteenth century occurred at the coal mine in Avondale, Pennsylvania. A fire broke out and the lack of air supply smothered 110 men and boys. New laws required changes in mining shafts, but there were no laws passed preventing children as young as ten years old from working in the mines.

OCTOBER 8, 1871 The Great Chicago Fire started in or very near the O'Leary barn. The fire, driven by a strong wind, headed straight for the center of the city. The fire was so hot that it took two days to assess the damage: more than 2,000 acres, 20 miles of streets, 120 miles of sidewalks, 18,000 buildings, and $200 million in property. The homeless totaled more than 200,000.

JUNE 24, 1876 General George Custer's 7th U.S. Cavalry was destroyed by Sioux Indians at the Battle of Little Big Horn, Montana.

SEPTEMBER 19, 1881 President James A. Garfield died of wounds from an assassin.

AUGUST 27, 1883 The explosion of the Krakatoa volcano, which was 26 times more powerful than the largest H-bomb ever tested. Krakatoa was an

uninhabited island west of Java. Debris shot 34 miles into the air and the noise was heard 3,000 miles away. The greatest damage occurred from the subsequent 120-foot high tsunami (tidal wave) that swallowed up about 163 villages and 36,000 residents in Java and Sumatra.

SEPTEMBER 2, 1885 During the Rock Springs Massacre, a mob of white coal miners attacked their Chinese co-workers in Rock Springs, Wyoming. The violence erupted during labor disputes at the mining camps. Chinese homes were burned and as many as 28 Chinese were killed. This was one incident in a series of race riots against Chinese immigrants.

SEPTEMBER 1887 The world's most devastating flood occurred when the waters of the Hwang Ho, or Yellow River, in China topped 70-foot levees. Water spilled over 50,000 square miles, wiping out 300 villages, killing between one and six million people, and leaving another two million homeless.

MAY 31, 1889 In Johnstown, Pennsylvania, a wall of a neglected dam split open, the resulting flood covering the town and surrounding villages. At least 2,000 lives were lost.

DECEMBER 20, 1890   The last American Indian battle occurred at Wounded Knee, South Dakota, where American soldiers massacred 200 Sioux men, women, and children.

JANUARY 17, 1893   Hawaii's monarchy was overthrown as a group of businessmen and sugar planters forced Queen Liluokalani to abdicate her throne.

JANUARY 8, 1894   Fire destroyed the Columbus World's Fair.

JULY 1894   Japan initiated the Sino-Japanese War.

JANUARY 5, 1895   French Captain Alfred Dreyfus, convicted of treason, was publicly stripped of his rank. (He was ultimately vindicated.)

MAY 27, 1896   The St. Louis/East St. Louis tornado, which was to be one of the deadliest in U.S. history, killed 137 people in St. Louis and created more than $10,000,000 in damage.

JUNE 12, 1897   The force of the great Assam earthquake in India destroyed buildings in Calcutta, 200 miles away. Its magnitude on the

Richter scale was 8.7 and the landslides and flooding that followed cost thousands of lives.

FEBRUARY 15, 1898   The U.S. battle-ship *Maine* mysteriously blew up in Havana Harbor, killing more than 260 crew members and bringing the United States closer to war with Spain. The Spanish-American war began in April 1898.

1899   British Troops in South Africa, over-whelmed by the hot climate, drank straight from rivers. Of 400,000 troops, 43,000 con-tracted typhoid.

DECEMBER 1899   During the "Black Week," British forces suffered three serious defeats in the Boer War against Dutch settlers in South Africa. The Boers eventually surrendered in May 1902.

The Twentieth Century

AUGUST 14, 1900   Western forces defeated the Boxer Rebellion, the fight of Chinese against foreign exploitation in China.

SEPTEMBER 6, 1901 President McKinley was shot and mortally wounded at the Pan-American Exposition in Buffalo, N.Y. by anarchist Leon Czolosz. Theodore Roosevelt became President of the United States.

JULY 31, 1902 In the worst mining disaster in Australia, lamps with naked flames caused an explosion and landslide at Mount Kembla, New South Wales, trapping 250 miners underground. The final death toll was 96.

DECEMBER 30, 1903 A month after the opening of the new, fireproof Iroquois Theater in Chicago, the scenery caught fire, killing at least 600 of the 1,900 people in the audience. Only 1 of the 500 performers and crew died. The building remained undamaged.

FEBRUARY 7, 1904 A fire in Baltimore raged for about 30 hours and destroyed more than 1,500 buildings.

FEBRUARY 10, 1904 The Russo-Japanese War began when Japanese torpedo boats attacked the Russian fleet in Port Arthur in northern

China. The Japanese emperor blamed the conflict on Russia's ambitions in Korea and Manchuria.

JUNE 15, 1904 When the three-deck side wheeler *General Slocum*, "Queen of the Excursion Steamers" caught fire soon after it departed from the pier at East Third Street in New York City, one of New York's biggest disasters occurred. The boat was carrying 1,335 passengers, most of them children. More than 1,000 passengers died, 124 were injured; only 160 escaped unharmed.

1905 Formation of Sinn Fein, the Irish Nationalist movement.

JANUARY 9, 1905 On "Bloody Sunday," Russian strikers and their families at the Winter Palace in St. Petersburg were fired on by Tsarist troops. The death toll was 500. The tsar was away for the weekend.

APRIL 4, 1905 A major earthquake in Lahore, India, killed more than 10,000 people.

1906   An outbreak of Bubonic Plague in India resulted in a quarantine called by the Second Indian Plague Commission.

APRIL 7, 1906   A terrifying flow of lava covered the Italian countryside after the eruption of Mount Vesuvius near Naples. Soot and ash from the sky fell on roofs, which collapsed under its weight.

APRIL 18, 1906   The San Francisco Earthquake, followed by raging fires, killed about 2,500 people. Huge fires raged all over and looters attacked the city. Martial law was declared.

DECEMBER 28, 1908   The Sicilian town of Messina was devastated by one of the most violent earthquakes recorded in European history. The earthquake created a tsunami, a massive sea wave, across the straits of Messina to mainland Italy.

FEBRUARY 1, 1908   King Carlos I of Portugal, 44 years old, was assassinated by a mob.

MARCH 25, 1911   The Triangle Fire occurred at the Triangle Shirtwaist factory in New York City. The fire raged for only half an

hour, but 141 workers—most of them young female immigrants—died of burns and suffocation or were killed jumping from windows.

JANUARY 18, 1912   English explorer Robert F. Scott and his expedition reached the South Pole, only to discover that Roald Amundsen had beaten them to it. Scott and his party perished during the return trip.

APRIL 15, 1912   The British luxury liner *Titanic* sank in the North Atlantic off Newfoundland, after striking an iceberg. The death toll was about 1,500.

FEBRUARY 3, 1913   The 16th Amendment to the Constitution, providing for a federal income tax, was ratified.

AUGUST 1913   The Mona Lisa was stolen from the Louvre Museum in Paris by an Italian waiter.

JUNE 28, 1914   Archduke Franz Ferdinand, heir to the Austrian throne, was assassinated at Sarajevo, starting a war between the Austrian Empire and Serbia, leading to World War I.

AUGUST 13, 1914 Germany declared war on France and invaded Belgium. This was the beginning of The Great War—the "war to end all wars."

NOVEMBER 14, 1914 The Ottoman sultan declared a holy war on the Allies.

1915 An earthquake in Avezzano, Italy, killed 30,000 people.

JANUARY 12, 1915 The U.S. House of Representatives rejected a proposal to give women the right to vote.

JANUARY 28, 1915 The United States lost its first ship in World War I, the *William P. Frye* carrying wheat to England.

JANUARY 31, 1915 Germany launched its first poison gas—chlorine—attack against the Russians. In April 1915 at Ypres on the Western Front, German troops unleashed their new weapon on Allied troops.

MAY 17, 1915 The passenger ship *Lusitania*, with almost 2,000 passengers aboard was attacked by a German U-boat off the coast of

Ireland. Although a passenger ship, the *Lusitania* was carrying a large cargo of war supplies. All those aboard perished.

OCTOBER 12, 1915 A German firing squad executed British nurse Edith Cavell, found guilty of helping British prisoners escape.

DECEMBER 4, 1915 Inspired by D. W. Griffith movie *The Birth of a Nation*, the Ku Klux Klan, banned in 1872, was re-launched in Atlanta, Georgia by William Simmons.

1916 America's worst polio epidemic hit in 1916, with 7,000 deaths and 27,363 cases reported. The largest outbreaks of polio reoccurred in 1949 and 1953. In 1955 the first polio vaccine was distributed in the United States.

FEBRUARY 21, 1916 Germany attacked the French City of Verdun in a siege that lasted almost one year. Germans suffered 434,000 casualties; French 542,000.

APRIL 29, 1916 The East Monday rebellion in Ireland was crushed by the British, destroying hopes for an independent Ireland.

JULY 1, 1916 In a single day during the Battle of the Somme, the British suffered 57,470 casualties in attacks on the Germans.

FEBRUARY 3, 1917 The United States liner *Housatonic* was sunk by a German submarine, causing diplomatic relations between the United States and Germany to be severed.

APRIL 16, 1917 The U.S. declared war on Germany.

MARCH 15, 1917 Tsar Nicholas II abdicated the Russian throne and the Russian Revolution began with rioting and strikes in St. Petersburg.

JUNE 13, 1917 A new German aircraft, the Gotha GV biplane, first bombed London, killing more than 100, including children.

1917 The French ship *Mont Blanc*, loaded with approximately 7000 tons of picric acid and carrying a deck cargo of gasoline high explosives, collided with another ship while entering the port of Halifax, Nova Scotia. Fire broke out onboard from gas ignited in the collision. Approximately one-half of Halifax was

leveled, a number of nearby ships were completely demolished, and the casualties amounted to 1,226 people dead and thousands of others injured.

JULY 17, 1918 The execution of the Russian royal family took place in the cellar of the house where they had been held. The Romanovs had ruled Russia since 1613.

1918 A worldwide epidemic of Spanish flu was the worst since the

Black Death. Total deaths were estimated at more than 20 million. In spite of its name, this flu did not begin in Spain but in the Middle East. In the U.S., the death toll hit more than 500,000 people.

JANUARY 5, 1919 The National Socialist Party (Nazi) was formed as the German Farmers Party.

MARCH 23, 1919 Benito Mussolini founded the Fascist Party in Italy.

JANUARY 2, 1920 During the Palmer Raids, 10,000 American union and socialist organizers were arrested.

JANUARY 16, 1920   Prohibition began in the United States as the 18th Amendment to the US Constitution took effect. (It was later repealed by the 21st Amendment.)

JULY 23, 1920   Assassination of Mexican revolutionary Pancho Villa.

NOVEMBER 21, 1920   The Black and Tan, members of British auxiliary police stationed in Ireland against the republicans, initiated "Bloody Sunday," to retaliate against the IRA's murder of 11 Englishmen suspected of being spies. The attack took place at a soccer match in Dublin, killing 12 and wounding 60.

October 30, 1922   Benito Mussolini, calling himself Il Duce, and an army of 24,000 Fascists marched into Rome. King Victor Emanuel was forced to declare Mussolini Prime Minister of Italy.

1923   The Ku Klux Klan claimed that its membership topped 1 million.

SEPTEMBER 16, 1923   Tokyo, the largest city in Japan, and Yokohama, its most important seaport, were devastated by an earthquake. As many as 300,000 people perished.

JANUARY 3, 1925   Benito Mussolini dissolved the Italian parliament and became dictator.

MARCH 18, 1925   A tornado struck north-northwest of Ellington, Missouri. For the next three and a half hours more people would die, more schools would be destroyed, more students and farmers would be killed, and more deaths would occur in a single city than from any other tornado in U.S. history. The tornado, which was classified at F5 and covered three states, Missouri, Illinois, and Indiana, set records for speed—62mph—and path length—219 miles. The death toll was 695 with a total of 2,027 injured.

MAY 25, 1925   John T. Scopes was indicted in Tennessee for teaching Darwin's theory of evolution. He was fined $100 and new state laws were passed forbidding the teaching of ideas that contradict Old Testament stories about the creation of the world.

 MAY 18, 1926   At the Bath School in Michigan, a school board member and farmer blew up the elementary school, killing 45 people, including 38 students. The bomber killed himself and the Bath School superintendent by blowing up his pickup truck.

JANUARY 10, 1928   The Soviet Union ordered the exile of Leon Trotzky.

FEBRUARY 14, 1929   The "St. Valentine's Day Massacre" took place in a Chicago garage as seven rivals of Al Capone's gang were gunned down.

OCTOBER 29, 1929   Black Tuesday on the New York Stock Exchange, when prices collapsed amid panic selling and thousands of investors were wiped out. This began America's Great Depression.

DECEMBER 27, 1929   As part of Stalin's Five-Year Plan, peasants in the Soviet Union were forced to give up their land and join collective farms. Many peasants opposed the collectivization program and destroyed their crops and killed livestock rather than hand them over. Resistors risked being sent to camps in Siberia. This was the beginning of the worst period of Stalin's rule of the Soviet Union, known for its purges of intellectuals, scholars, and political leaders, its brutal prison camps and extreme hunger .

JANUARY 4, 1932   British East Indies Viceroy Willingdon arrested Gandhi and Nehru.

MAY 12, 1932 Aviator Charles Lindbergh's baby was found dead after being kidnapped on March 2. Bruno Hauptmann went on trial in 1935 in Flemington, New Jersey, on charges of kidnapping and murder charges. He was found guilty and later executed.

JULY 8, 1932 The stock market fell to its lowest point during the Depression.

JANUARY 30, 1933 Adolf Hitler was named chancellor of Germany

AUGUST 1, 1933 The German Reichstag passed a law giving Adolf Hitler dictatorial power.

AUGUST 19, 1934 A plebescite in Germany vested sole executive power in Adolf Hitler as Führer.

OCTOBER 21, 1934 Mao Tse-tung's "Long March" began in China. The Communists marched northwest from Kiangsi to Yan'an, about 6,000 miles away. They reached Yan'an after marching for 368 days, but one third of the 100,000 marchers were killed in the first three months of the march.

1935 Mao Tse-tung gained control of the Chinese Communist Party.

SEPTEMBER 29, 1936 Civil War erupted in Spain. Francisco Franco assumed power.

MAY 6, 1937 The German dirigible *Hindenburg*, filled with hydrogen, burned and crashed in Lakehurst, New Jersey, killing 36 of the 97 people aboard.

1937 Adolf Hitler ordered the construction of Buchenwald concentration camp.

JULY 2, 1937 Aviator Amelia Earhart disappeared over the Pacific Ocean while attempting to make the first around-the-world flight at the equator.

AUGUST 13, 1937 At the outbreak of the Wusung-Shanghai campaign on August 13, 1937 and in front of the watching eyes of the American and British navies and many Europeans and Americans, the Japanese army used poison gas against

Chinese troops. In the succeeding eight years of war, Japan had used poison gases in 14 Chinese provinces 1,131 times. Biological warfare is not new. The first recorded use of biological agents in war dates to the Romans using dead animals to foul the water supply of the enemy and the Tartars catapulting bodies infected with bubonic plague over the city walls of Kaffa to kill its enemies. The modern history of biological warfare began in 1918 when the Japanese formed Unit 731 of its army, dedicated to the development of germ warfare. The United States and Great Britain soon began biological and chemical warfare development. During the twentieth century, biological, chemical, and germ warfare was used extensively, reaching its height during the Vietnam War, and in recent wars in developing countries, particularly in the Middle East. There are currently efforts to have a global ban on all kinds of biological and chemical warfare.

 AUGUST 23, 1937 Italian-born anarchists Nicola Sacco and Bartolomeo Vanzetti were executed in Boston for murders during a 1920 robbery. They were vindicated in 1977.

NOVEMBER 10, 1938 The streets of Berlin and other German cities were strewn with broken glass, after a night of terror named Kristallnacht. More than 7,000 Jewish shops were wrecked and looted, hundreds of synagogues burned, and Jews beaten up by uniformed Nazis.

SEPTEMBER 1, 1939 Nazi Germany invaded Poland, officially beginning World War II.

SEPTEMBER 14, 1939 Nazi German and Fascist Italy signed the "Pact of Steel" to become a full-fledged military alliance. Mussolini had wanted to call it the "Pact of Blood."

SEPTEMBER 3, 1940 The Nazis began their first experiments using gas chambers at Auschwitz. In January of 1942, mass killing using Zyklon-B gas was instituted.

SEPTEMBER 7, 1940 Germany began its blitz on London. The blitz caused enormous damage and cost the lives of more than 43,000 civilians— 139,000 more were injured. It did not, however, force England to surrender.

AUGUST 1941 The Siege of Leningrad began, during which more than 650,000 people died of starvation. The city was bombed and cut off from all supplies and medical aid during the siege, which lasted 900 days.

SEPTEMBER 29, 1941 The largest single death squad killed 30,000 Jews at Babi Yar, a ravine near Kiev.

DECEMBER 7, 1941 Japanese warplanes attacked the U.S. Pacific fleet at Pearl Harbor, Hawaii, leading to America's entry into World War II on December 8th.

DECEMBER 11, 1941 Germany and Italy declared war on the United States.

JANUARY 20, 1942 Nazi officials held the notorious Wannsee conference, during which they arrived at their "final solution" that called for the extermination of the Jews.

APRIL 9, 1942 This was the starting day of the Bataan Death March, the forced march of 70,000 American and Filipino prisoners of war captured by the Japanese. They were force-marched 55 miles, starved, mistreated, beaten, and shot along the way. Only 54,000 reached their destination of Camp O'Donnell. Lieutenant General Homma Masaharu was charged with responsibility and tried by a U.S. military commission in Manila in 1946. He was executed.

FEBRUARY 3, 1943 After being torpedoed by a German submarine, the Allied troopship S.S. *Dorchester* sank, losing 600 lives, among them four chaplains now honored by Congress, which named the date "Four Chaplains Day."

AUGUST 4, 1944 Anne Frank and her family were discovered in their secret annex in Amsterdam and arrested. Anne Frank died in the Bergen-Belsen concentration camp in March 1945, before her sixteenth birthday.

DECEMBER 16, 1944 This day marked the start of the Battle of the Bulge, which ended a month later with 77,000 Allied casualties.

FEBRUARY 3, 1945 Flying Fortresses— almost 1,000 of them—dropped 3000-ton bombs on Berlin.

FEBRUARY 13, 1945 Beginning on the night of February 13th and continuing until April 17, Anglo-American forces conducted massive bombing raids by 800 aircraft on the city of Dresden, Germany. The raids obliterated the greater part of one of Europe's most beautiful cities, killing between 35,000 and 135,000 people.

MARCH 9, 1945 Tokyo was hit by U.S. napalm bombs and 80,000 people died in one night.

APRIL 29, 1945 American soldiers discovered Dachau concentration camp, near Munich, Germany, with 39 box cars filled with corpses. The total estimated dead in the Holocaust was 11 million.

JULY 30, 1945 The USS *Indianapolis* was torpedoed near the Pacific Island of Tinian just after delivering components for the first atomic bomb. Only 316 out of 1,196 men survived. Many who died were eaten by sharks.

AUGUST 6, 1945 The United States dropped an atomic bomb on Hiroshima, Japan to end World War II. It was the first use of a nuclear weapon in warfare and killed an estimated 140,000 people.

AUGUST 9, 1945 The United States exploded a nuclear device over the innermost portion of Nagasaki, Japan, killing between 60,000 and 80,000 people.

MARCH 22, 1945 In Cairo, this date marked the formation of the Arab League, a regional organization of Arab States in the Middle East aimed at strengthening the political, cultural, economic, and social programs of its members. In spite of objections from Jordan, the league admitted the PLO—the Palestine Liberation Organization—as the representative of all Palestinians.

APRIL 16, 1947 The French ship *Grandcamp*, carrying ammonium nitrate fertilizer, caught fire and blew up in the harbor of Texas City, Texas. Another ship, the *Highflyer*, exploded the next day. The explosions and resulting fires killed more than 500 people and left 200 others missing.

JANUARY 30, 1948 Indian political and spiritual leader Mahatma Gandhi was murdered by a Hindu extremist, Nathuram Godse. Gandhi, who in 1947 had won India's freedom from British rule, was shot while walking to a prayer meeting with his grandnieces.

MAY 14, 1948 Formation of the State of Israel was followed by Arab League attacks.

MAY 28, 1948 The National Party in South Africa, which backed a policy of apartheid, won a victory in the all-white general election.

OCTOBER 1, 1949 Mao Tse-tung declared the establishment of the People's Republic of China, causing Chiang Kai-Shek's nationalist government, supported by the United States, to flee.

 JANUARY 17, 1950 The Brink's office in Boston was robbed of $1.2 million in cash and $1.5 million in securities by 11 robbers.

JANUARY 21, 1950 Former State Department official Alger Hiss, accused of being part of a Communist spy ring, was found guilty in New York of lying to a grand jury. Hiss, who always maintained his innocence, was sentenced to prison.

FEBRUARY 22, 1950 The first allegations were made by Wisconsin Senator Joseph McCarthy that at least

205 employees of the State Department were card-carrying members of the Communist Party. This opened the doors for a "reign of terror," promoted by Anti-Communist fear, causing many prominent Americans, including famous writers and Hollywood stars, to lose jobs and face persecution.

JUNE 25, 1950 The Russian-equipped North Korean army invaded South Korea, initiating the Korean War. Korea, surrendered by the Japanese at the end of World War II, had been divided in two, each half maintained by Soviet and U.S. forces. When armed conflict began in December, the "Cold War" between the U.S.S.R. and the U.S. heated up.

1950 South Africa's national government passed The Population Registration Act, making apartheid legal. South Africans were required to carry race identification cards.

JULY 20, 1951 King Abdullah of Jordan was assassinated in Jerusalem.

NOVEMBER 1, 1952 The United States exploded the first hydrogen bomb in a test in the Marshall Islands.

1956 USSR forces invaded Hungary to suppress Anti-Communist rebellion.

JULY 25, 1956 The Italian ocean liner *Andrea Doria* sank after a collision with the Swedish ship *Stockholm* off the New England coast, killing 51 people.

JANUARY 1, 1959 Fidel Castro led Cuban revolutionaries to victory over Fulgencio Batista.

FEBRUARY 3, 1959 Three top rock 'n' roll stars, the Big Bopper, Buddy Holly, and Richie Valens all died in a plane crash.

MARCH 21, 1960 Police in Sharpeville, South Africa—near Johannesburg—fired on blacks protesting racial pass laws. The result, known as the Sharpeville Massacre, was 72 deaths and over 300 injuries in two days of violence.

MAY 1, 1960 The Soviet Union shot down an American U-2 reconnaissance plane, capturing its pilot, Francis Gary Powers.

JANUARY, 1961 The U.S. broke diplomatic relations with Cuba.

APRIL 17, 1961 CIA-trained Cuban exiles launched the disastrous Bay of Pigs invasion of Cuba in an attempt to overthrow the government of Fidel Castro.

AUGUST 15, 1961 Work began on the Berlin Wall, sealing off the city's eastern and western sectors.

JANUARY 30, 1962 Two members of the "Flying Wallendas" high-wire act were killed when their seven-person pyramid collapsed during a performance in Detroit, Michigan.

JANUARY 14, 1963 George C. Wallace was sworn in as governor of Alabama with a pledge of "segregation forever."

NOVEMBER 22, 1963 President John F. Kennedy was assassinated while riding in a motorcade in Dallas, Texas. Lee Harvey Oswald—who had shot the president from the Texas Book Depository building—was later shot by Jack Ruby.

1964 President Lyndon Johnson sent the first U.S. troops to Vietnam. U.S. forces reached a peak of 543,000 in 1969.

JUNE 21, 1964   Three civil rights workers disappeared in Philadelphia, Mississippi. Their bodies were found six weeks later and although eight members of the Ku Klux Klan went to prison, none served more than six years.

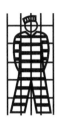

1965   Black muslim leader Malcolm X was gunned down.

AUGUST 11, 1965   Rioting and looting broke out in the predominantly black Watts section of Los Angeles. During the riots 34 people were killed and more than 1,000 injured.

NOVEMBER 5, 1966   After 40 hours of rain in Europe, two-thirds of Florence, the cultural capital of Italy, was under six feet of water. The River Arno burst its banks, and mud and slime covered some of the world's greatest paintings, sculptures, mosaics, and frescoes. Damage was estimated at about $80 million.

JANUARY 27, 1967   Astronauts Virgil I. "Gus" Grissom, Edward H. White and Roger B. Chaffee died in a flash fire during a test aboard their *Apollo One* spacecraft at Cape Kennedy, Florida.

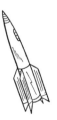

JUNE 5, 1967   The third clash between Arab and Israeli forces since World War II came to be called the Six-Day War. Israeli retaliation

for Syrian bombardments of Israeli villages came
on June 5, when the Israeli Air Force shot down
six Syrian MiG planes. During this short war,
Israel eliminated the Egyptian air force, and
gained the Old City of Jerusalem, the Sinai and the Gaza Strip, the
Jordanian territory west of the Jordan River known as the West Bank,
and the Golan Heights on the Israeli-Syrian border.

JANUARY 30, 1968 On the Tet holiday,
when many South Vietnamese soldiers
were home on leave, an estimated 84,000
North Vietnamese Communist troops
invaded South Vietnam cities, attacked
government installations, and even gained
entrance to the American embassy in Saigon. The Tet Offensive was
costly to the Communists, but turned the tide of the war against the
U.S. and was instrumental in the eventual withdrawal from Vietnam.

MARCH 16, 1968 The My Lai Massacre in Vietnam was carried out
by U.S. troops under the command of Lt. William L. Calley Jr.'s
Charlie Company. They attacked the small village of My Lai, later

discovering that the villagers were unarmed and the battle was in reality a massacre. Lieutenant Calley was put on trial for murder connected with the incident and sentenced to life at hard labor.

APRIL 4, 1968   The Reverend Dr. Martin Luther King, on a visit to Memphis, Tennessee, was killed by a sniper's bullet while standing on the balcony of the motel where he was staying. On March 10, 1969, the accused white assassin, James Earl Ray, pleaded guilty to the murder and was sentenced to 99 years in prison.

JUNE 5, 1968   Senator Robert F. Kennedy was shot and killed just after winning the California Democratic presidential primary. He spoke to his followers in Los Angeles' Ambassador Hotel, and as he left through a kitchen hallway he was fatally wounded by a Palestinian immigrant, Sirhan Bishara Sirhan.

APRIL 13, 1970   The *Apollo 13* exploded en route to the moon, 200,000 miles from earth. The lunar landing was cancelled and the crew did arrive safely back on earth.

MAY 4, 1970   Ohio National Guardsmen opened fire on anti-war protesters at Kent State University, killing four students and wounding nine others.

JANUARY 2, 1971   At the end of a soccer match in Glasgow, Scotland, a barrier collapsed at Ibrox Park football ground, killing 66 people.

JANUARY 8, 1971   At San Clemente Island, California, 29 pilot whales beached themselves and died.

FEBRUARY 2, 1971   Idi Amin assumed power in Uganda, following a coup that ousted President Milton Obote. During his military dictatorship, Amin expelled all 70,000 Ugandan Asians, many Israelis, seized foreign-owned businesses, and ordered the killing of an estimated 300,000 people. Amin was overthrown in 1979.

JANUARY 30, 1972   Thirteen Roman Catholic civil rights marchers were shot to death by British soldiers in Northern Ireland on what became known as "Bloody Sunday."

JUNE 17, 1972   Five men--including James W. McCord Jr., security director for the Committee for the Re-election of the President (Nixon)--were arrested at the Watergate office building in Washington, D.C. on charges of breaking into Democratic National

Committee headquarters. Soon, G. Gordon Liddy and E. Howard Hunt Jr., two others with connections to the president, were linked to the break-in. This was the beginning of the Watergate scandal. The defendants were convicted and prosecutors then began to dig further into the incident. Top White House aids like John Dean, John Ehrlichman and H. R. Haldeman received prison sentences. The Watergate affair and its cover-up led to the resignation of President Richard Nixon on August 9, 1974. Gerald Ford was sworn in as president on the same day, and on September 8, 1974 issued a pardon for Nixon "for all offenses against the United States which he…has committed or may have committed."

SEPTEMBER 5, 1972   Arab guerrillas attacked the Israeli contingent at the Munich Olympic games, killing 11 Israelis. Five guerillas and a police officer also died.

OCTOBER 6, 1973   On the Jewish holy day of Yom Kippur, Israel was attacked by Egypt across the Suez Canal and by Syria on the Golan Heights. Israel and Egypt signed a cease-fire in November and a peace agreement in January 1974.

JANUARY 2, 1974   The worst fire in Argentine history destroyed 1.2 million acres.

1974   A massive earthquake in China killed more than 200,000.

1974   Cyclone Fifi struck Honduras, claiming 10,000 lives.

FEBRUARY 29, 1975   More than 40 people were killed in London's Underground when a subway train smashed into the end of a tunnel.

JANUARY 24, 1978   A nuclear-powered Soviet satellite plunged through Earth's atmosphere and disintegrated, scattering radioactive debris over parts of northern Canada.

NOVEMBER 18, 1978   The religious cult, the People's Temple, committed mass suicide under orders from their paranoid leader Jim

Jones. More than 900 were found dead at their Jonestown, Guyana commune. Most drank a cyanide-lace fruit drink, and those who refused to drink were shot.

JANUARY 30, 1979   The civilian government of Iran announced it had decided to allow Ayatollah Ruhollah Khomeini, who had been living in exile in France for 15 years, to return.

MARCH 28, 1979   The nuclear accident inside Unit Two at the Three Mile Island plant near Middletown, Pennsylvania was America's worst.

APRIL 10, 1979   A tornado more than one mile wide hit Wichita Falls, Kansas, leaving 42 dead. It was one of 13 tornadoes to touch down in one day in Texas and Oklahoma, and remains one of the most damaging tornadoes in American history.

NOVEMBER 4, 1979   The Iranian hostage crisis began as militants stormed the United States Embassy in Teheran.

1980   An American attempt to free 53 hostages held at the American Embassy in Iran resulted in the deaths of eight members of the rescue squad.

MAY 18, 1980   The Mount St. Helens volcano in Washington state exploded, leaving

57 people dead or missing. The volcano, which had been dormant since 1857, collapsed, and then exploded, blasting ash with a temperature of 572°F. Fortunately, the area had been closed off, but still more than 60 people died and 70 square miles of wildlife were destroyed. The explosion also set off an avalanche, moving tons of snow at 250 miles per hour.

DECEMBER 8, 1980   Beatles star John Lennon was shot outside his home at the Dakota apartment building in New York City. A memorial to Lennon called "Strawberry Fields" was created in Central Park at 72nd Street near the Dakota.

JANUARY 28, 1981   The tanker *Olympic Glory* spilled 1 million gallons of oil in a collision with a ship at Galveston Bay, Texas.

OCTOBER 6, 1981   Egyptian President Anwar Sadat was shot to death by extremists while viewing a military parade.

JANUARY 13, 1982   An Air Florida 737 crashed into Washington D.C.'s 14th Street Bridge after takeoff and fell into the Potomac River, killing 78 people.

MARCH 2, 1982   Argentina invaded the Falkland Islands off the coast of South America to take control back from Great Britain.

OCTOBER 13, 1983   American troops invaded the Caribbean island of Granada.

OCTOBER 23, 1983   A suicide truck-bombing at Beirut International Airport in Lebanon killed 241 U.S. marines and sailors; a near-simultaneous attack on French forces killed 58 paratroopers.

OCTOBER 31, 1984   Indian Prime Minister Indira Gandhi was assassinated near her residence by two Sikh security guards.

DECEMBER 3, 1984   At midnight, over 40 tons of poisonous methyl isocyanate gas leaked from Union Carbide's pesticide factory in Bhopal, India. Thousands died in the immediate incident, and since then, at least 10,000 more have died. Other victims suffer from breathlessness, brain damage, immune diseases, and more. A settlement of $470 million from Union Carbide was accepted in 1989, as compensation for the death toll and surviving victims.

1985 A state of emergency was declared in South Africa following violence resulting from new laws excluding black representation in politics.

JANUARY 13, 1985 An express train in Ethiopia derailed, killing at least 428 people.

AUGUST 20, 1985 Just after dawn, letter carrier Patrick Sherrill reported to work in Edmond, Oklahoma, a town of 35,000 north of Oklahoma City. His mailbag concealed two loaded .45-caliber pistols. In silence, he first shot the supervisor in the chest at close range, and in the next ten minutes shot 50 rounds, killing 14 employees. Finally, he shot himself. This was one of the first post office massacres that raged through the United States in the 1980s and 1990s.

NOVEMBER 13, 1985 Colombia's Nevado del Ruiz volcano had been active for a few months, but since the activity was limited to mudslides on its slopes, the town of Armero was not evacuated. The

volcano finally erupted, spewing hot ashes onto glaciers, which then formed a river of debris and black ash nearly 13 feet deep, burying the town of Armero and killing 22,000, about 90 percent of its population.

OCTOBER 7, 1985   Members of the Palestinian Liberation Organization (PLO) hijacked the Italian cruise ship *Achille Lauro* in the Mediterranean with more than 400 people on board. One of its passengers, an American, was murdered. This was retaliation for an Israeli bombing attack on PLO headquarters near Tunis.

JANUARY 28, 1986   The space shuttle *Challenger* exploded 73 seconds after liftoff from Cape Canaveral, killing all seven crew members.

APRIL 26, 1986   A reactor in a Soviet Union nuclear plant in Chernobyl exploded. At least 31 people died immediately and radioactivity entered the atmosphere, causing severe illness and unknown damage.

OCTOBER 19, 1987   The Dow Jones Industrial Average, amid frenzied stock market selling, plunged 508 points— its biggest one-day decline in history.

DECEMBER 21, 1988 A terrorist bomb exploded aboard a Pan Am Boeing 747 over Lockerbie, Scotland, killing all 270 people aboard.

MARCH 24, 1989 America's worst oil spill took place when the supertanker *Exxon Valdez* ran aground on a reef in Alaska's Prince William Sound, leaking 11 million gallons of crude.

JUNE 4, 1989 Chinese army troops stormed Tiananmen Square in Beijing during a pro-democracy movement. Casualties were in the hundreds, perhaps thousands.

JANUARY 7, 1990 The Leaning Tower of Pisa in Italy was closed to the public after leaning too far.

FEBRUARY 7, 1990 An 811-foot tanker, the *American Trader*, spilled hundreds of thousands of gallons of Alaskan crude oil off the coast of Huntington Beach, California.

OCTOBER 16, 1990 The first killer bee hive was seen in Texas. *Apis mellifera scutellata*, or Killer Bees, originated in Africa and migrated to Brazil in the 1960s. In the 1970s they arrived in Central America.

The bees were the result of experiments to combine European bees with Africanized bees to improve honey production. Bees in the experiment escaped and developed into an aggressive breed. Killer bees in Texas and surrounding area were labeled dangerous and put in quarantine. As of May 2000, killer bees were migrating into Arizona. Although the sting of these bees is no more powerful than ordinary bees, killer bees attack in groups of thousands and have caused at least four deaths.

JANUARY 7, 1991   Operation Desert Storm began the Gulf War, and Iraq fired SCUD missiles on Israel.

JUNE 15, 1991   Mount Pinatubo, about 55 miles north of Manila in the Philippines, had been dormant for 600 years, when it threw millions of tons of ash 50,000 feet into the air. Tropical rains turned the ash

to mud, and the catastrophic landslides are thought to have killed 550 people, destroyed 50,000 acres and lost half a million people their means of living.

APRIL 1992   Nationalist Serb snipers fired on peaceful demonstrators in Sarajevo, marking the beginning of the War in Bosnia. In 1990-1991

when Croatia and Slovenia declared their independence from the Yugoslav Federated Republic, a bloody conflict began between ethnic Serbs and Croats in which cities in Slavonia were leveled by bombardment and about one-third of Croatian territory was occupied. Warfare was halted by the United Nations, but violence continued. The clash has continued with reports of "ethnic cleansing" and other crimes of humanity, massacres, bombing raids, and other atrocities.

APRIL 29, 1992 Deadly rioting broke out in Los Angeles after a jury acquitted four Los Angeles police offers in the videotaped beating of Rodney King. The rioting killed 54 people and caused $1 billion in damage.

AUGUST 24, 1992 Hurricane Andrew caused record damage in Florida, Louisiana, and the Bahamas, and was blamed for 55 deaths.

FEBRUARY 26, 1993 A bomb exploded in the garage of the World Trade Center in New York City, killing six people and injuring more than 1,000 others.

APRIL 19, 1993 After a 51-day siege and shoot-out that erupted near Waco, Texas, when U.S. Federal agents tried to serve warrants on the Branch Davidian cult members, at least 70 cult members were believed dead. David Koresh, leader of the

Waco group, a rock guitarist from Dallas who had preached a gospel of sex, freedom and revolution, died of a gunshot wound.

OCTOBER 1993   In a remote Vietnamese hamlet, 53 villagers committed suicide with guns and other weapons. A local man, Ca Van Liem, convinced the tribe that suicide would bring a quick trip to paradise and took cash donations for a guarantee.

JANUARY 17, 1994   A 6.7 magnitude earthquake struck Southern California, killing at least 57 people and causing billion of dollars in damage.

SUMMER 1994   Rwandan Tsutsis butchered a million of their Hutu neighbors in Africa.

OCTOBER 1994   Police found the burned bodies of 48 Solar Temple members in Switzerland. Solar Temple is an international sect believing in rebirth through ritualized suicide.

JANUARY 17, 1995 More than six thousand people were killed when an earthquake with a magnitude of 7.2 devastated the city of Kobe, Japan and the neighboring industrial centers of Osaka and Kyoto. This was the worst earthquake in Japan in 50 years, and the death toll numbered 5,000.

MARCH 20, 1995 In Tokyo, Japan, packages containing the poisonous gas sarin were deliberately leaked on several subway trains, killing 12 people and sickening more than 5,500 others.

APRIL 19, 1995 A truck bomb exploded outside the Federal Building in Oklahoma City, killing 168 people and injuring 500. Timothy McVeigh was convicted of the bombing and sentenced to death.

OCTOBER 3, 1995 O.J. Simpson was acquitted of the 1994 murder of his former wife and her friend.

DECEMBER 1995 In a burned house outside Grenoble, France, 16 members of the cult Solar Temple were found dead.

July 16, 1996   TWA Flight 800 to Paris crashed moments after take-off from Kennedy Airport in New York. All 230 aboard are killed.

March 26, 1997   Thirty-nine people were found dead lying on their backs and covered with purple shrouds. The victims, who died by poison, were found in a home in Rancho Santa Fe, an exclusive community north of San Diego. The group was known as Heaven's Gate and members believed that after their deaths they would rendezvous with a UFO traveling behind the Hale-Bopp comet.

August 31, 1997   After a high-speed car accident that occurred in an underpass near the Place de l'Alma in Paris, France, Diana, Princess of Wales, was pronounced dead.

February 3, 1998   A U.S. military plane accidently clipped cable car lines in northern Italy, killing 20.

July 17, 1998   Three tsunamis, waves created by a submarine earthquake, rose 30 feet, destroying seven villages in Papua, New Guinea. Residents were swept into inhospitable jungle and swamp. The death toll amounted to about 4,000, approximately half the local population.

JULY 20, 1998 Monsoon rains caused the Ganges River in Bangladesh to break its banks, leaving eight million people homeless. Many areas stayed under water for two months, and after the flood receded, the World Health Organization reported that as many as 20 million people would suffer from flood-related diseases such as malaria, dysentery, ear and eye infections, and skin problems.

APRIL 20, 1999 Two students set off pipe bombs and went on a shot-gun rampage in Columbine High School in the well-to-do suburb of Littleton, Colorado. By the end of the rampage 12 students, one teacher, and both gunmen were dead, and 23 others wounded.

JULY 16, 1999 John F. Kennedy, Jr., his wife, and his sister-in-law all died when the private plane he was piloting crashed in the Atlantic Ocean.

AUGUST 1999 A 45-second earthquake in Northwest Turkey killed 17,000 people and flattened 60,000 buildings.

NOVEMBER 3, 1999 The worst mass killing in Hawaii's history occurred in an office building in Honolulu when a Xerox technician opened fire on other employees. Seven victims were all shot at close range by a 9mm handgun. Another killing took place in Seattle the

next day, when a gunman shot and killed two men in
a shipyard office. These were only two in a rash of
incidents, including one in a Connecticut Lottery
office in 1998, one in a General Motors office in

Florida, and one by a day trader who attacked two Atlanta, Georgia
brokerage firms in July 1999. These shootings brought attention to
workplace assaults and spurred studies of why people suddenly explode
at work. It also brought more lobbying efforts at handgun control.

DECEMBER 1999   At the Venezuelan port of La Guaira near Caracas,
massive landslides caused by heavy rain left 150,000 people homeless,
and it is estimated that 30,000 more died, buried by mud or washed
out to sea.

DECEMBER 1999   By the end of the year, the total
world population infected with AIDS stood at 33
million, 23 million of them in sub-Saharan Africa.
The U. S. toll reached almost half a million.

MARCH 18, 2000   The death toll and source of a chemical fire
among a Ugandan doomsday cult remain unknown. The cult, known
as the Movement for the Restoration of the Ten Commandments of
God, had a compound and church in the village of Kanangu. Many
members were found dead in a ritual mass suicide that is believed to
have predated the fire and the bodies of others exhumed from the
area might have been murdered.

JUNE 20, 2000   A customs search at Liverpool, England of a Dutch truck importing tomatoes revealed the bodies of 58 Asian men and women. It was presumed that the Asians were poor immigrants being smuggled into Britain who had died of suffocation from heat and lack of ventilation. The doors of the truck had been locked from the outside and refrigeration equipment shut off.

SUMMER 2000   The United States experienced its worst wild land fires in 50 years, with 76 large fires raging in 13 states. The estimate of land damage was at 4.7 million acres.

JULY 25, 2000   Less than one minute after takeoff from Charles de Gaulle airport, a Concorde jet crashed in a Parisian suburb, killing all 109 passengers as well as four people on the ground.

AUGUST 12, 2000   A Russian Oscar II-class nuclear submarine performing exercises in the Barents Sea, became crippled by technical faults and sank to 450 feet beneath the surface, with 118 men aboard. Rescue efforts failed and all aboard perished.